EC's Number One Fan
The Historic 1950s Fanzine Writing of Larry Stark

I0132476

Boardman Books

August 2016

Bartlett, Tennessee

©2016 Boardman Books

EC's Number One Fan: The 1950s Fanzine Writing of Larry Stark (*Comics Monographs* #4) is published by Boardman Books. Edited and prepared for publication by Matthew H. Gore. All Rights Reserved. No part of this book may be reproduced or transmitted in any form or by any means, electronic or mechanical, including photocopying, recording, or by any information storage or retrieval system, without permission in writing from the publisher. For information address Boardman Books, 8062 Jills Creek Drive, Bartlett, Tennessee, 38133. Introduction ©2016 Thommy Burns. All other textual content ©2016 Larry Stark. Layout, cover design, and incidentals ©2016 Boardman Books.

Ruby Kast & Nancy Siegel, 1952 (by Marie Severin)

First Signed & Numbered Limited Edition: June 2016
Open Edition: August 2016

ISBN-13: 978-0692741931
ISBN-10: 0692741933

AN ENTERTAINING COMIC

EC

Elegy to "Elegy"

by Thommy Burns

Larry Stark's "Elegy" to EC Comics was originally published in seminal EC fanzine *HOOHAH!* #6 (September 1956). It has since been reprinted in *The Complete EC Checklist* (1963, 1970, and 1974 editions) and in *Tales Of Terror!* (2000) and *American Comic Book Chronicles: The 1950's* (2013). "Elegy" is a passionate remembrance of something truly meaningful to its author: EC's inspired "New Trend" in comics - the revolutionary output of the Entertaining Comics Group, 1950-55. It is tinged with the bitterness of recent loss, and gilded with the afterglow of recent glory. It is, quite simply, the single greatest piece of commentary written during the Golden Age of comics. To understand it's importance, one must understand the uniqueness of the creator-to-fan relationship fostered and enjoyed by the EC faithful in the early 50's. EC did not produce expendable, inconsequential "junk" - they produced fine art, worthy of study, of criticism...of devotion. Larry Stark knew quality, he knew good writing and art, and he responded in kind. Larry wrote a detailed letter of criticism on every single issue of EC's "New Trend" and in return he was given a free lifetime subscription to "everything we publish" by Bill Gaines, who also bestowed upon Larry the title of "EC's Number One Fan".

Sometime in the middle of 1956, Pat Armstrong, president of a *MAD* fan club based in Alexandria LA, suggested that *HOOHAH!* publisher Ron Parker "try and get an article out of Stark" for his fanzine - with five issues completed and virtually all of EC's Big Name Fans contributing Larry was notable in his absence. Armstrong provided Larry's address and Ron wrote to him in hopes that "EC's Number One Fan" would provide something print worthy. Ron later figured that "Stark had probably not even heard of *HOOHAH!* when I wrote him, but the immediate result was 'Elegy'." An offhand request for a submission had garnered the single best remembered and most highly regarded piece to ever appear in an EC Fanzine. "Stark never wrote anything else for *HOOHAH!*", Ron would remember, "but, then, he didn't have to. Classics, after all, are tough acts to follow."

This is the first publication of the original typescript of "Elegy". It is reproduced here from a copy sent to Larry by Gaines, who owned the original. After its initial publication in *HOOHAH!* #6 Ron Parker sent the original manuscript to Bill Gaines, who told Larry years later that he had saved it. They met at a comic convention in New York and Bill asked Larry if he wanted it. Larry said the words and not the paper were important to him, and that if he could have a Xerox of it Bill could keep the original. "I hope it's important to you," Bill told Larry, "because it's important to me." Ron Parker recalled in an article for *Squa Tront* in 1983 that "Elegy" was "probably the greatest article that ever appeared in an EC fanzine. There is little doubt that *HOOHAH!* #6 was the best of the issues, and 'Elegy' was its nucleus. . .it contained sadness, for Larry's article expressed the finality of it all. There was little to be said after 'Elegy'."

The original, unedited typescript is presented here with the permission of both Stark and Parker.

MAD
485 MADISON AVENUE
NEW YORK, NEW YORK 10022

"Elegy"

MAD
485 MADison Avenue
N. Y., N. Y. 10022

FIRST CLASS

Larry Stark
41 Bowdoin St. #54
Boston Ma 02114

The return envelope for "Elegy."

13 Serviss Avenue
Route #9
New Brunswick
New Jersey
Friday, 27 April, '56
1500 Hours

E L E G Y

"Let us sit upon the ground,
And tell sad stories
Of the death of kings."
——W.Shaxpy

EC is gone. Nothing remains but a memory, and the tattered copies
yellowing in the closets of collectors. For EC death was long and
cruel in coming, and almost as undeserved as it was inevitable. The
meteor of its genius was hot and brief, yet flashed with such a
brilliance as to make forgetting difficult.

I suppose I was a normal introvert throughout adolescence,
delaying maturity with an over-attention to books, reading almost
anything and deciding later about its worth. Rather soon after beginning
high school ~~comicxbooks~~ I found comic books had become slightly
amusing diversions, though a little below the dignity of any honest
interest. They merited an occasional orgy, but piles of perused magazines
rated little but contempt. Then, about the ~~beginning~~ middle of my senior year
(early 1950), Entertaining Comics began to appear on the newsstands
in their 'New Trend' format, and my careful intellectualism had to
undergo a modification.

So far as I could see, EC began the use of fantasy and science-
fiction in the comic field, though everyone jumped on both bandwagons
immediately. EC magazines, though, were the only comics of any variety

3

that I wanted to read a second time; they were the only comics I could read straight through, without my mind clogging with cliches and rebelling somewhere in the middle. That is, they were written well. Compared to competitors, EC's were Pulitzer Prize material, and compared with similar material in contemporary pulps...or even by the masters of writing...they displayed a care and craftsmanship that the field did not seem to deserve.

I had been writing almost constantly for two or three years, more amateurish fiction than anything else, and always managing to finish stories with one grand spark of inspiration. During that senior year, and the next summer, I seemed to run out of flint. Happily, however, I'd absorbed half a dozen collections of radioplays by Arch Oboler and Norman Corwin, and spent some time with the Speech and Drama Department, and met some enthusiastic friends. During that xxx summer, when ideas refused to flow, I spent my time fooling with a recording-machine, and grinding out an occasional adaptation of an EC story in radioscript form. The bare minimum of facilities, the grand style of the men I'd taken as models, and an appreciatory belief in the sacredness of the words I was transcribing...all of these conspired with my inexperience to create some pretty outlandish scripts.

The year of personal drought did accomplish some things for me, though. I learned how to handle conversation. I built up a tendency to suggestion and evocation, rather than dull, direct plotting. I managed to get through an idea-less dessert without really having stopped writing. I probably learned a little bit about story structure. And, most important to this account, I came on intimate terms with the ideas and expressions of EC's staff of writers, and learned to appreciate their power and imagination.

The drought lasted, more or less, through my first year of college. I took a full five-subject schedule, went at night, arose late and loafed most of the day. The following summer I did the adolescent

4

equivalent of 'running away from home': I spent the summer with relatives in Upstate New York, and arranged to go to college there during the following year...also at night, also with concomitant loafing-time available.

During that summer I mailed three things to professional editors. The first was a pretty putrid spaceship-story(with no conflict and not much else), which subsequently acquired half a dozen rejection-slips; the others were two "sample-scripts", stories of my own devising, sent to Harvey Kurtzman "to illustrate the kind of story I would prefer to see in TWO FISTED TALES and FRONTLINE COMBAT" (the two comics he ~~edited~~). Harvey mailed them back, with a note explaining that all EC material was staff-written, but noting that they were "Very realistic. Not like usual comic-book material." It was undoubtedly the kindest and friendliest editorial reaction I've ever seen.

Thrilled over being noticed at all, I worked out a very lengthy critical-essay on what I'd liked and hadn't liked in the issues of TFT and FC that I'd bought. THAT letter was answered, briefly, with thanks and interest. Both letters from Harvey were on the back of the standard EC reply-sheet, along with the detachable subscription-blank, and I proceeded rather slowly to extend my few subs to all of the (then eight, I think) titles. Also, I began spilling my spleen over two to four pages of letter in comment on each new issue by H.K., and writing in the tone of an almost-equal and a friend. That's how he'd made me feel. By the beginning of the school year Upstate, I'd finally paid for subs to all titles, and as they began arriving on a regular schedule, I took the plunge and began writing "Mr. Feldstein" about new-and-past issues of the magazines he edited. That must have made a profound impression on everyone at the office.

Along about January of 1952, a neatly typed letter signed Bill Gaines arrived Upstate. It sed they liked the fact of my commenting, and agreed with only half of it. It admitted to stealing from a number

5

of sources that I'd pointed out. And it casually mentioned that my
name had been entered on a list ㎙for Free Subscriptionship Membership
in EC for life. I don't think that dulled my critical fangs too much,
but it certainly made my hat a dozen sizes too small. For the next
year or two, until well into the Crash, I don't think I missed an
issue with comment of some kind, most usually three or four pages
of criticism, appreciation, and notation of literary larceny.

When I arrived home from that year of college Upstate, a letter
was forewarded to me. It was from Jerry Dee, a member of Harvey's
staff. Jerry did research-work for the war-magazines, and had been
writing the one-page text-fillers that went into the centerfold of
each of Harvey's publications. He was about my age, liked his job
and his associates as well as any fan, and had a burning desire to
write. We carried on quite a lively and interesting correspondance
for some time. Mixed in with advance-info on stories, office-gossip,
notes on artists, techniques of drawing, comparative criticisms of
associates, and notes on the general situation of comics, Jerry used
to include an occasional proof of up-coming pages; had I had anything
but a passive interest in fandom then, EC fandom might easily have
become something of genuine importance. I had a pipeline direct to
the scene of the crime.

EC remained, in my opinion, the best-written comic magazine line
ever published...and periodically topped itself with new plateaus of
excellence. There were a number of "house-plots" and cliches, more-so
toward the end of the period, but always some unexpected peak of
originality would make the whole thing worth waiting for. At their
best, EC was easily on a par with the best pulp-fiction available.
And, if specific individual stories were considered, many of them
were a good deal better, both in originality of concept and completion
of expression. ㎙㎙㎙ Al Feldstein and ~~Georg Kurtzman,~~ Bill Gaines, ~~and his things~~ Harvey Kurtzman, and
Johnny Craig, gave their creations much more than they would seem worth.

And they did it on phenominal schedules. Feldstein was required to turn out better than a story every ~~week~~ _day_ for four years, together with conducting conferrences with artists, and doing layout-work on most of the pages. Kurtzman had a less straining schedule, but he justified it by doing a preliminary-sketch of each panel, and cramming his magazines with so much research, his illustrations with actual photographs used as guides, that everyone admitted the accuracy of detail was unimpeachable.

It would also seem to be a general rule that every artist who joined EC on a permanent basis inevitably showed exceptional ~~~~ maturity and improvement of style. Wally Wood drew things into comic-panels that no man would seem capable of. Joe Orlando ultimately turned out entire stories drawn so well and so distinctively that he rivalled even Wally. Jerry remarked once that EC had work from every top artist in the business except Reed Crandall...and during the early days of the crash even he joined the staff. There is more good art in the pages of EC publications than in the entire output of the rest of the industry for the same period.

The secret of the triumph, I think, is that almost everyone felt free when working with EC, and that instead of satisfying either an art editor or a collection of readers, everyone attempted to satisfy their own personal ideas of excellence.

In September of '52, I made a visit to the office. I stayed four hours, and talked to practically everyone around. It seemed a joyous occasion on every hand, though there were hints of impending doom. Marie Severin described "day after day when nobody speaks to anyone", and "people screaming at one another"; Feldstein and Gaines mentioned that the "~~Summer~~ _Spring_ slump" hadn't picked up yet; Al Feldstein lapsed a few times into an edgy pessimism over "knocking yourself out doing what you think is great material, when you know damn well it isn't going to sell, and it isn't selling."

But I was in no mood to notice the hints of impending doom. I gabbled for an hour with Marie about the artists, and for a couple of hours with Bill about the how's of writing, editing, and comic-art. I gloried in the special sign over Bill's desk "God help us to write stories that will please Larry Stark" (Made by Marie, and stored in my closet even now); I sat in on a conference with George Evans about his art, and listened to Bill proof-read some finished pages aloud. I hung on after everyone m left, while Bill emptied a drawer and showed me the posters and cockeyed-covers that were decorations at the previous Christmas office-party; and when I left at six o'clock, my feet hardly touched the pavement.

It seemed that the Happy Times left the office with me that afternoon. Within the next month, Jerry reported that comic-titles were folding at the rate of one and two a week; kmxx a few months later, that comic COMPANIES were folding one andm two a week. The "Summer slump" turned into a major economic crisis....and yet EC plunged rather xxxbkkxx steadily through it all. Somehow, their reputation for excellence must have acquired more lasting readers. During the early uneasiness, EC not only remained in business, they added titles to their list, and added artists km to their staff.

But there were nasty corners. Jerry Dee wrote one war-story, and was allowed to write text-fillers for all EC titles; then, perhaps because of the economic pinch, Bill gave the fillers to an outside writer. Jerry asked me to pan the new writer, hoping it would help him get the job back again. Though the new stuff was poor, it didn't help Jerry.

Johnny Severin, with a lot of general experience doing 'American Eagle' scripting for PRIZE, argued often and bitterly with Kurtzman over art, and probably over story-content. Jerry preferred Severin's ideas to Harvey's autocratic ideas on editorship.

Jerry mentioned once a situation that was ultimately to ruin the

—whole industry. "Those two iconoclasts in the other office have gone overboard on a story about baseball." Jerry thought the emphasis on gory detail was out of place. The story was "Foul Play", one of Dr. Wertham's prime exhibits in the later comic-investigations.

The truth was, Bill and Al were getting a little worn thin from the constant demand for stories; they had slipped into a rut of sadism and grue, a formula which seemed to sell comics much better than anything else. Their frazzled imaginations, plus the income-curve which dipped steadily farther down and ultimately nosedived, combined to make writing so much an ugly, unpleasant chore, and "house-polts" began to predominate the horror field. The only variation, then, was in the details of the stories, and these were getting bloodier and bloodier. Never totally unimaginative, Feldstein fell back into doing ingeniously original descriptions of gruesome scenes, caring less and less for any objective or personal standards of excellence. The whole industry was overstocked with horror, most of it had to be raw and cheap, and even those who had once poured more art than blood into their writing could no longer think of artfully concieved stories. When the industry came under official scrutiny, they had no defense.

At the end, the happy crew I had known was pretty well broken up. Jerry ran himself ragged carting books from Brooklyn to Kurtzman's home, so that Harvey might still work while recovering from yellow jaundice. He joined a couple of the artists who wrote their own stories for Harvey's magazines during that time, and then left the comic industry entirely. Severin, after THE NEW TWO-FISTED TALES collapsed, had already left EC. That title itself was edited by a new man, after Harvey's brilliant war-stories failed to pay for themselves. Kurtzman was left with MAD alone.

In the other office, Bill Gaines stopped taking an active part in the plotting-sessions, and finally for the last half-dozen issues almost everything Feldstein edited was written by outsiders. Looking over old issues, it's almost possible to point out precisely where everyone stopped caring how good their work was. Almost everything seems the same, but the soul is missing.

I don't think I exaggerate when I say some of the best writing I've read has been found in EC comics. Aside from the tightrope-like assignment of writing such short, limited stories on such a schedule, EC stories always managed to acquire a distinctive flavor, a personal style, and a magnificently wide scope. If any popular writing deserves a claim as to literature, this does also. They were, at their best, mature conceptions totally explored, and with a constant attitude toward realism and honesty mixed in with the short, sharp crackle of drama.

And, ultimately, I think it was EC's general excellence that killed it, on all levels. I was always one to argue that even a comic-writer has a duty to write as best he is capable of writing, and by his own inner conviction of what constitutes proper art and excellence. However, I must admit that it seems unwise to sell Faulkner, Caldwell, and McCullers to seven-year-olds. Insofar as these writers had a duty to themselves to finish these kinds of stories with integrity, they also had a duty to choose the correct kind of story to tell. As things turned out, the best writer of sensationalism and perversion was also the worst writer, judged from a different framework.

Also, the general economic situation forced the excellence of EC to loop back and destroy itself. In order to be as good as they were, these people demanded appreciation. They simply didn't get it from the comic buyers. Trash sold as well as EC; even better, because its creators weren't worth Kurtzman's or Feldstein's salaries. And, when the public stopped buying, they didn't cut back judiciously, but stopped buying all comics in general...denying these artists and writers the satisfaction of knowing their sweat and perfection was recognized and appreciated. Once the crash forced EC to recognize that they were regarded as just another comic-publisher, all incentive to keep working and trying failed them. Al Feldstein's bitter comments, both in '52 and last December, were those of a man who felt acutely the lack of an appreciative audience.

Finally, I think in the last stages of the degeneration, all of EC's staff felt it something of a blow to their pride to have to turn out their work on such a grueling schedule, and without thought to excellence. Once the glow of pride left the office, and the job became one of supplying a set number of pages per month, regardless of quality, I think most of those people felt some kind of shame at what they were creating.

I know rather little about the "New Direction" kick, or the "Picto-Fiction" idea, though I've been back to EC twice since that first visit. When I arrived the next time, even the number, size, and arrangement of offices had been changed, and practically everyone did their work somewhere other than at the EC offices. There was new personnell around, and those few familiar people either didn't sound the same, or didn't have time for discussions. Now... I'm not even sure there IS an office any more. But I'm not sure I would enjoy revisiting my friends; it might turn out too much like a wake.

Still, I've had a rare privilege. I was allowed to know EC, intimately, at its prime. I knew most of the staff, not personally, but professionally, more thoroughly than I've known most of my classmates at school. I've laughed at their private jokes, ~~exxxxxxx~~ ~~xxxx~~scolded at their failures, brooded over their errors, and soared in praise of all they accomplished with integrity and excellence. I've probably had more experience as a kind of critic than would ever be possible in so short a time, and I'm certain that alone has helped mold whatever amount of personal style I possess. This organization has done a lot for me, and meant a lot to me. When I felt their -interest failing, I felt embittered too. When the censors chopped

their work to shreds for impossible reasons, I added my hate to
their fires. They are my friends, a crew of the best persons and
personalities, the most enjoyable creators I've been allowed to meet.
I hope this final economic deathblow will not be a complete end, either
of EC, or of my connection with my many friends there. I thrived in
the reflection of their glory, and shared in their pride of accomplishment.
They will not be easy to forget.

Finished 2030 Hours.

'Fess up, Mr. P.... Was Pat Armstrong
a relative of "Mrs. Arlene Grandon Phelan & sisters"? In other words, a fake?

Anyway, here's something.

I like Hh.... a little. My complaint:
everything is too damn short, and that is a
compliment in disguise. Seems to me that
your writers can think of very little of importance
to say, & so say whatever tiny tidbits they
have very briefly.

WHY will articles of fact stir
update? OPINIONS stir debate, Ron, not
inside info & undisputable facts.

I like your humor-piece; nicely
carried & executed. Goodwin is okay, too, though
his story is a little long & cliché-ridden getting
to the fairly good conclusion; good luck — but don't
expect too much from me. EC is dead & I'm editing Stellar
with White.

Cheers, Larry

12

Notes on "A Perfect Nightmare"

by Thommy Burns

In his 1954 book Seduction Of The Innocent, Dr. Fredric Wertham asserted that comic books could not be considered literature because all great literature inspired scholarly and thoughtful criticism, and comics did not. Bhob Stewart was incensed, and thought immediately of the EC criticism of Larry Stark. Stewart decided to edit a new publication "not as a fanzine but as a literary journal of the kind then known as 'little magazines'. " Handily, fellow fan Ted White had a mimeograph machine that printed postcard sized pages and *POTRZEBIE* was born. Taking its name from a Polish word sprinkled throughout the pages of *MAD*, Stewart envisioned *POT*, as it was sensibly abbreviated, as a forum for Larry's EC reviews. In the first editorial Stewart wrote that "POTRZEBIE'S main purpose in life is to present the criticism of Stark...sans censorship. You rarely get to peruse his monstrous prose other than a few sentences in the EC letter columns. EC values his opinions so much that Gaines has given Larry a free lifetime subscription to all the EC Comics on the condition that he will write EC a letter about each issue telling what he liked and didn't like about it. Now you'll know too. Thru POTRZEBIE." Stark's column was titled ONE MAN'S OPINION, subtitled A COLUMN OF CRITICISM. This first column consisted of detailed reviews of *Two Fisted Tales* #38 and *Haunt Of Fear* #25.

Also in that first issue of POT was a script by Stark, written as if for a radio play, titled "A Perfect Nightmare For Nancy Siegel". In *Squa Tront* #7, in an installment of his EC Fanzine history, John Benson wrote that "A Perfect Nightmare" was "a piece of fan fiction written in the form of a radio script, complete with well placed instructions to the sound engineer. The first scene takes place at the EC offices, with Larry himself dropping in, ostensibly to deliver his monthly letter of criticism in person, but actually to wangle a date with Nancy Siegel." He goes on to say that the piece is a "quite successful attempt to recreate the lighthearted atmosphere of the EC offices" and indeed it is, having been based on Larry's first hand observations of a story conference between Bill Gaines and Al Feldstein, the interaction between brother and sister John and Marie Severin, and the back-and-forth as Harvey Kurtzman and Jerry DeFuccio hashed out the details of a war story. Larry first visited the EC offices in Sept. of 1952 which is also the date on his original typescript for "A Perfect Nightmare", making it entirely probable that the piece was written immediately following his first visit, while the details were fresh! Almost 65 years later it gives the reader a tantalizing glimpse of the day to day goings-on at 225 Lafeyette St., Room 706, written by one who was there! The story has a very EC-twist-ending, which I won't spoil here.

One interesting, and major, change the original typed pages reveal is that the piece was originally titled "A Perfect Nightmare For Ruby Kast"! Nancy and Ruby both worked in the EC offices in the early 50's, and when I asked Larry the reason for the change he said: "I just needed a female character for the plot and the twist ending, and the more I thought about it, I decided Nancy was closer in age to me. I had no idea she would be marrying Bill Gaines in a few years!"

PERFECT   NIGHTMARE
f
o
r

Nancy Seigel

b
y
STARK

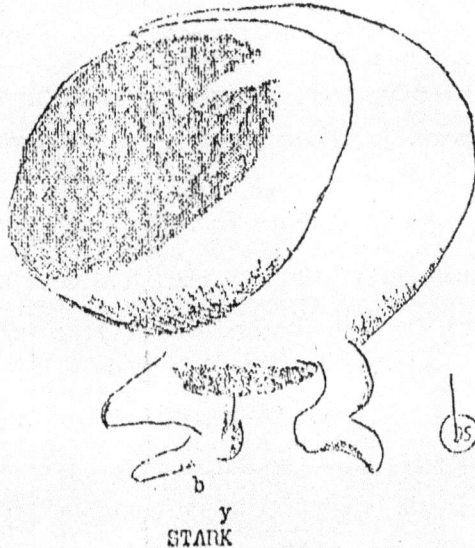

SOUND: FADE IN A GENERAL HUBUB OF CONVERSA-
TIONS, ETC., FROM ACROSS MR. LEE'S OF-
FICE, PERHAPS THE HOWL OF A SOUL IN
MORTAL TORMENT (IN REALITY H. KURTZ-
MAN TRYING TO VERBALIZE THE MATING
CALL OF A SUBMARINE BELL-HORN), PRO-
MINENT CLACKING OF SHIRLEY'S TYPEWR-
ITER, AND THE ON-MIKE VOICES OF MR. G.
AND MR. F. CREATING A "NEW" EPIC LIKE
SO:
Al: So, there's these two partners, see—
make 'em coal-mine owners...
Bill: —who prefer to save money by not us-
ing safty equipment.
Al: Exactly. An' a rabble-rouser's trying
to fire up the men to start organized
Union methods, wants 'em to walk out
because anybody with half a mind would-
n't send men into the lower east dig-
gings so soon after the cave-in last
week...
Bill: —that buried poor ol' Harry and his ac-
cordeoon.
Al: Jus' then up pops these two partners,
makin' fun of the whole idea about—
Bill: The Haunted Shaft. Write that down,
looks like a good title. "I never ordered anyone to do anything I wouldn't
do myself!"
SOUND: DOOR OPENS.
Al: And so they— they—
Bill: Oh, hi Larry. What brings you around?
Larry: Just killing time for an appointment

ABOVE: Perfect Nightmare as originally published in POTRZEBIE #1, with a first page illustration by Bhob Stewart.

night...
MUSIC: HIGH MINOR CHORD, MOSTLY BRASSES, SICK-
CUE.
Nancy (Screams!): LARRY!!!
Larry (deliberate, demoniacal, possessed): At
midnight... I... turn into... a... wolf!!
SOUND: VICIOUS SNARLING ROAR FROM LARRY, BLE-
NDED AND MIXED WITH A STOCK RECORD OF A
LARGE BRONX-ZOO-TYPE LION DEFENDING HIS
LEFT HIND ZEBRA-LEG FROM ALL COMERS. GROWS
SWIFTLY ON MIKE, SUSTAINS THROUGH
Nancy: S H R I E K S ♪♪♪♪♪♪
SOUND: D
E
A
D
SILENCE.

Well, kiddies, that's
our boy Stark for you!
Always ready with
a surprise for the
girls! Bet Nancy
was a little sur-
prised. Hear she
was a little late
for work the next
morning. More of
Stark in ZIP #s 5
and 6; 5¢ apiece...
The Cess-Pool Cleaner

LEFT: The final page of A Perfect Nightmare as published in POTRZEBIE #1, with GhouLunatic style closing patter by the "Cess Pool Cleaner!"

NANCY
SIEGEL

JUST ONE?

RUBY KAST

Saturday-Sunday, 6-12-13-14 September, '52
Penn.R.R.Train, & Route #9
New Brunswick
New Jersey
(SCRIPT)

9 Pages

Perfect Nightmare
for ~~Ruby Kast~~ Nancy Seigel
by
Stark

SOUND: FADE IN A GENERAL HUBUB OF CONVERSATIONS, ETC., FROM

   ACROSS MR. LEE'S OFFICE, PERHAPS THE HOWL OF A SOUL IN

   MORTAL TORMENT (IN REALITY H. KURTZMAN TRYING TO VERBALIZE

   THE MATING-CALL OF A SUBMARINE BULL-HORN), PROMINENT CLACKING

   OF ~~NANCY'S~~ SHIRLEY TYPEWRITER, AND THE ON-MIKE VOICES OF MR. G. AND

   MR. F. CREATING A "NEW" EPIC LIKE SO:

Al: So, there's these two partners, see---make 'em coal-mine owners...

Bill:--who prefer to save money by not using safety equipment.

Al: Exactly. An' a rabble-rouser's tryin' to fire up the men to start

   organized Union methods, wants 'em to walk out because anybody

   with half a mind wouldn't send men into the lower east diggings

   so soon after the cave-in last week--

Bill: That buried poor ol' Harry and his accordeeen.

Al: Jus' then up pops these two partners, makin' fun of the whole

   idea about---

Bill: The Haunted Shaft. Write that down, looks like a good title.

   "I never ordered anyone to do anything I wouldn't do myself!"

SOUND: DOOR OPENS.

Al: An' so they-- they--

Bill: Oh, hi Larry. What brings you around?

Larry: Just killing time for an appointment cross-town-- Thought I'd

   bring the 'Crypt' review in person. Keep right on throttling

   each other, I don't want to interfere.

Bill: That's what this place needs, Al: some critics with Courage!

Al: A few more with Courage and we're out of business. Ah--- Was

   delivering a review all you stopped in for, Larry?

Larry: Well,---- I thought maybe-- That is, I'd expected,---

SOUND: TYPING STOPS.

Nancy(With a smile in her voice): She's in the Stock Room, Larry.
Shirley

Larry: Thanks, ~~Nancy~~ *Shirley*. I'll file a report on my progress on the

 way out.(fading)

Bill: About the third date in a month, isn't it?"

All: Fourth-- IF he makes it. Well, anyway, these two partners---

 (FADE)

SOUND: GENERAL B.G. OF STOCK ROOM AND ADDRESSING ENVELOPES. DISTANT

 HOWL OF A SOUL IN MORTAL TORMENT (J. DEE TRYING VALIANTLY BUT

 VAINLY TO RECREATE THE ENTIRE BROOKLYN NAVY YARD WELCOMING

 HOME THE "Franklin", ORCHESTRATED FOR SOLO VOICE)

Larry: ~~Ruby~~ *Nancy*.....?

SOUND: ADDRESSING CEASES.

~~Ruby~~ *Nancy*: Huh? Oh, Larry. Hi.

Larry:Like the aide of a male right arm on that thing? Here-- I'll

 crank and you feed. ~~(Haven't any idea what sound it makes,~~

 ~~but for plot-purposes it works easier with two operators.)~~

Marie Severin(Detaching herself from low B.G. and floating on-

 mike): Say, there he is now! (on) Since when do critics enter

 this office without bowing to everyone?

J. Powers Severin: Hi, Larry.

Larry: Hi, Johnny. Now, Marie, you know I'd get to you eventually.

Marie: A left-handed compliment at best, but accepted. (remembers)

 Oh, say! Here's that original 'Hey Look' you wanted me to

 steal from Harvey.

Larry: Great. --- Uh, could you file it in the note-pad? I seem to

 be rather occupied.

~~Ruby~~ *Nancy*: And you're getting good at it, too, with all this practice.

Johnny(picking up an EXIT cue): Well, we have some----

Marie: Oh, say, I've got them plates for the new MAD yarns by

 Woody and this poor brute here. I'll let you---

J.P.: 'S a story set in the Cave Man Days, Larry. You know---

when if a man wanted a woman removed-- well, he just...

Marie(slightly screaming): Johnny! John-EEE, Put me down!

J.Severin: See you later, Larry.

Nancy
Ruby & Larry: FADE OFF-MIKE BUT PROMINENT,LAUGHING. J.P. AND SISTER
    STAY ON-MIKE THROUGHOUT THE FOLLOWING.

Marie: JOHN-EEEEE!

Johnny: There!

Marie(rallying a counter-attack and angry):Johnny Severin, if you
    ever do that to me again, I'---

Johnny: Listen, sister dear, can't you get it through your empty
    little head that there are times when the conversation of
    THREE people becomes just a bit superfluous?

Marie: Huh??

Johnny: Oh, for gosh sakes, listen then!

Marie(the dawn comes up like thunder): Oh, you mean---?

Johnny(A Born Evesdropper): Ssh!!

Larry(Low and slightly off- mike): I did have a bit more in mind
    than practice turning cranks, Ruby.

Nancy
Ruby: And what might that be?(KEEP THESE TWO OFF-MIKE)

Al(ON-mike): What's going on out here?

Bill: Holding a caucass?

Marie(whispers): Sssh. Just listen.

Larry: The stock opening, I suppose, is 'Are you doing anything
    tonight?'

Shirley
Nancy(coming on, full): Is she--- ?

Evesdroppers(FOUR!):Sssshh!

Shirley
Nancy(whispers): --hooked y et?

Nancy
Ruby: Well, I had planned to stay at home and relax tonight. It's
    been a rough week.

Harvey(Up): Is anything the ----

Marie(whisper):Ssh! We can' t hear.----- And YOU be quiet, too!!

Jerry(Whispers): But I didn't SAY anything!

Larry: Can't I change your mind? This may be my last chance for

a while,-- And I promise you'll be back before midnight this

time. Word of honor.

~~Ruby~~ Nancy (tactful, but unwilling):I-- I don't think so, Larry, I--

Marie(Arguing, full up, unable to keep silence any longer): Why not?

~~Ruby~~ Nancy (startled): What??

Marie(Cheer-leading before the aggregation): She's been out with

him before, right??

Staff: Right!

Marie: And admitted she enjoyed herself?

Staff: Right!

Marie: And hasn't dated anyone else since?

Staff: Right!

Marie: Then why not tonight ?

Bill: Good idea, ~~Ruby~~ Nancy. You've seen enough of him on office time,

how about buttering up the critics after hours?

Sen. John P. Severin: Madam Chairman, I request a poll of the

delegation!

Marie: All those in favor of ~~Ruby Kast~~ Nancy Seigel giving Larry a date tonight

say 'Aye!'

Staff: A Y E !!

Larry: Well, ~~Ruby~~ Nancy?

~~Ruby~~ Nancy (Overwhelmed by the onslaught, but laughing): Okay, I know when

I'm voted down-- Aye! But I was outnumbered!

Staff: Breaks into disjointed cheering, snake-dances off-mike to
CAPS
wake up Johnny Craig and report the results of the election.

Marie: I'll expect my usual fee in the morning's mail, sir.

~~Ruby~~ Nancy: Can't a gal even try a bit of feminine wiles around here?

Marie: When we need a satisfied critic, never!!

MUSIC: SHORT BRIDGE. FADES INTO

SOUND: DESERTED STREET JUST OFF WASHINGTON SQUARE, WHERE THE

SILENCE IS DELICIOUS, THE STREET-LIGHTS DIM OUT OF COURTESY,

AND THE SIDEWALKS NARROW ENOUGH TO DEMAND COZINESS.

FRENCH HEELS AND MALE BROGANS, SLOW AND DREAMY AND THOUGHTFUL,

AS IF STILL UNDER THE SPELL OF SOMETHING VERY BEAUTIFUL.

SERVE AS RYTHM SECTION FOR

~~Ruby~~ Nancy (Whispers softly, almost inaudibly, breathing the words into

existence as if not daring to spoil what memory is recreating).

Roses love sun shine.   Vi'lets love dew.

Angels in hea ven—

SOUND: DEEP, SELF-SATISFIED , LUSCIOUS SIGH.

~~Ruby~~ Nancy (breathless): Oh, gee, but that was beautiful!

Larry: I'm so glad you liked it.

~~Ruby~~ Nancy (still captured): Such--- Such power! I still don't see how

they did it on that little stage. It--- It was beautiful!

Larry: Thomas Bouchet could have been played a little better, though.

I've seen---

~~Ruby~~ Nancy (amused): The Eternal Critic!! Oh, but even with the rough

spots, it was my favorite.

Larry: My favorite, too. And one reason I wanted especially to take

you out tonight. It's the last performance of 'Down In The

Valley' this season, and-- and I wanted you to see it. I feel

so happy you liked it.

~~Ruby~~ Nancy: It was wonderful.-- This whole Evening's been wonderful; the

dinner, and then that impossible little nightclub! Larry, how

on earth did you find a real "The Crypt" in New York?

Larry: Professional secret. What did you think of Maestro Romoff?

~~Ruby~~ Nancy: You mean at The Champaign Room? Oh, he was priceless. But

why didn't you tell me he played at the theatre, too?

Larry: And spoil the effect ? Oh, no. I've had more fun just

watching you tonight than you did.

~~Ruby~~ [Nancy] ~~Xxxxkxxxxxxxxxxxxxxxxxxxrmxxxxxxxx~~: Well, it's been a perfect

evening. Still is! (Gentler, leaning closer to mike) Just

cool enough to be cozy,-- and look. Even a full moon! Did you

arrange that, too?

Larry: Not that. If it'd been left up to me we'd never see a full

moon together. Besides, I promised you'd be home by midnight,

and it must be close to that now.

[Nancy]
~~Ruby~~: But why so early? I didn't mind last time, really.

Larry: Oh, hasn't anyone told you that yet. Every full moon-lit

night at midnight I grow fangs and turn into a wolf.

[Nancy]
~~Ruby~~(REAL close, softly, smiling): I'd say your fangs show a little

bit already!

SOUND: FOOTSTEPS HALT ABRUPTLY. THREE SECONDS DEEP, ECSTATIC

SILENCE. FINALLY BROKEN BY

[Nancy]
~~Ruby~~:Sigh.

Larry(heavy whisper, in close): Mind very much if I say I love you?--

because it looks like I do.

[Nancy]
~~Ruby~~: It-- It looks like I do, too.

SOUND: ABSENCE OF SAME. ANOTHER DISCREET, POINTED SILENCE, ENDED IN

THE USUAL WAY, AND FOOTSTEPS RESUME, MUCH SLOWER, AIMLESSLY

[Nancy]
~~Ruby~~: I--- I didn't think it'd happen this way, so soon, so

unexpected---

Larry: Not unexpected. I should have guessed the first time I

talked to you, how wonderful it made me feel. That's why

I had to be with you tonight---no matter what. I want you

involved and connected with everything that I've ever thought

perfect or beautiful in my life.

[Nancy]
~~Ruby~~: Like 'Down In The Valley'?

Larry: That especially--- a sweet, breathtaking tragedy of love.

[Nancy]
~~Ruby~~: It's so powerful and emotional.-- I almost cried a couple of

times.

Larry: I think I did, the first time I saw it.-- A privilege I

pay for when purchasing the seat.

Nancy
Ruby (amused): Row six, on the aisle--

Larry: --Critic's Seats.

Nancy
Ruby: Oh, I'm so glad I came tonight. And remember--- I almost didn't!

Larry: Remind me to find the staff the biggest box of candy in

all creation.

Nancy
Ruby: Such a wonderful night! Oh, I wish it'd never end. It's--

I've never felt like this before.

Larry: I wish it'd last forever, too--- but it looks like it

can't last too much longer. How about giving my wrist back

so I can see the time.

Nancy
Ruby: Oh, no! Not--- Not yet. Can't we forget about time for a

while. I don't want anything to spoil this.

Larry: I wouldn't want to for the world, Ruby, but---- Well, it

can't be helped. I-- I took a chance for this night-- a big

chance. (sincere) And it's been worth it, really. But, if

I don't---

Nancy
Ruby: Chance? What do you mean?

Larry: It's--- It's something I can't explain. You'll have to trust

me, just this once. There'll be other nights--other perfect

nights for us both. But it must be way past eleven already,

and---

Nancy
Ruby: But what's so important about midnight?

Nancy
Larry: Ruby, listen to me. I-- I love you more than I ever believed

I could love anyone in the world. You're the most precious

thing that's ever been given me in my life, and I'll let

nothing--- Nothing harm you.

Ruby (impressed & uncomfortable): Why--- Why, Larry. Of course,

if it means so much--- -

Larry: We'd better find a cab before---

SOUND: DIM, LOW, BUT AUDIBLE CHIMES IN SOME FAR-OFF TOWER.

MUSIC: VERY LOW AND ALMOST UNNOTICEABLE, AN OFF-BEAT CHORD,

    STRIDENT, HARSH AND BITING.

Larry(shocked, in discomfort): What's that? Wha--

   Nancy
~~Ruby~~(amused & relieved): There! It's twelve already, and nothing

    horrible's happened! Now let's forget this silly---

Larry: Twelve? Oh, no, not yet! Dear God in Heaven, not yet!!

Ruby: Wha---?

SOUND: CHIMES HAVE CONTINUED.

MUSIC: SECOND CHORD, ~~XXXX~~ SIMILAR, PYRAMIDED, FULL STRINGS, A

    BRASS OR TWO, DIFFERENT MINOR KEY.

Larry(Frantic): Come on! I--- I've GOT to find a cab! There MUST be

    a cab somewhere!

SOUND: BEGINS HURRYING ALONG STREET.

   Nancy
~~Ruby~~:Larry! What's come over you??

SOUND: CHIMES ARE FINISHING.

                                                     Danse
MUSIC: FINAL FULL-ORCHESTRA CHORD, LIKE SOMETHING OUT OF ~~DANSE~~

   Macabre
   ~~MACABRE~~, VERY HARSH, SUSTAINS.

                                        Nancy
Larry: The subway, then-- Hurry! Run, ~~Ruby~~! In God's name, Run,

    before it's too late! RUN!

   Nancy
~~Ruby~~(completely bewildered): Are-- Are you hurt? Larry, if I

    can--- Larry. Oh, Larry!.

Larry(labored breathing, in despiration): ~~Ixxx~~ You-- You should

    never have come. -- I didn't-- want this to happen--- I--

                                  Nancy
    I don't want to hurt you, ~~Ruby~~! Dear God, I don't WANT to

    hurt you! But----- at midnight--

MUSIC: HIGH MINOR CHORD, MOSTLY BRASSES, SOCK-CUE.

   Nancy
~~Ruby~~(Screams!): LARRY!!!

Larry(deliberate, demoniacal, posessed): At midnight-- I-- turn

    into-- a -- wolf!!!

SOUND: VICIOUS SNARLING ROAR FROM LARRY, BLENDED AND MIXED WITH

    A STOCK RECORD OF A LARGE BRONX-ZOO-TYPE LION DEFENDING

    HIS LEFT HIND ZEBRA-LEG FROM ALL COMERS. GROWS SWIFTLY ON

    MIKE, SUSTAINS THROUGH

Nancy
~~Ruby~~: <u>S H R I E K S</u> !!!!!

SOUND: D
                 E
                   A
                     D
                          SILENCE.

          —30—

www.ingramcontent.com/pod-product-compliance
Lightning Source LLC
Chambersburg PA
CBHW080939040426
42443CB00015B/3478